IMAGES
of England

MIDDLETON
THE SECOND SELECTION

IMAGES
of England

MIDDLETON
THE SECOND SELECTION

Hannah Haynes and Geoffrey Wellens

TEMPUS

Acknowledgements

Middleton Library for the use of some photographs and the help of Pat, Maria and Jean, which was very much appreciated, as was that of Harold Cunliffe, Carl Goldberg, the late Derrick Catterall, Alan Clegg, Roger Colson, Joan Gillett, T. Brown, Les Ward, Robin Ansell, the *Middleton Guardian*, Entwistle Thorpe & Co. Ltd, Ian Howard, Ken Haynes and others too numerous to mention, who lent photographs or helped in any way.

Frontispiece: Horridge's, the well-known electrical shop in Old Hall Street, being decorated to celebrate the coronation of Queen Elizabeth II in 1953. A fitting start to this book as it will be published during the Queen's Golden Jubilee Year. The shop closed in April 2001 on the retirement of Mike Horridge and his sister, Joy Lucas (see page 117) whose father, Councillor Arthur Horridge, was mayor in 1953.

First published 2002

Tempus Publishing Limited
The Mill, Brimscombe Port,
Stroud, Gloucestershire, GL5 2QG

© Hannah Haynes and Geoffrey Wellens, 2002

The right of Hannah Haynes and Geoffrey Wellens to be identified as the Authors of this work has been asserted by them in accordance with the Copyrights, Designs and Patents Act 1988.

British Library Cataloguing in Publication Data.
A catalogue record for this book is available from the British Library.

ISBN 0 7524 2647 8

Typesetting and origination by Tempus Publishing Limited
Printed in Great Britain by Midway Colour Print, Wiltshire

Contents

Awaiting King George V and Queen Mary, 1913, the town's first royal visit (see also page 14). Middleton Council recommended a general holiday, with St Leonard's church bells ringing from 12.30p.m. The fences are for the safety of the vast crowd. Children received a commemorative medal and the entire event was recorded on cine film.

Introduction

The Industrial Revolution brought many changes, not least the invention of photography, which meant that images of new developments could be recorded. In the last 150 or so years there has probably been more visual change than in all the years that preceded them. This was especially true of Middleton, where the last of the Asshetons, Lords of the Manor, were opposed to leasing land, which meant that the town was late in being developed. By the 1850s many towns had professional photographers, who often combined their new skill with talents as artists or trades such as shopkeepers and chemists. Middleton had four brothers; Robert, John, David and Samuel Jackson of Jumbo, working from the late 1850s, and examples of their work are identified in this book. Rhodes had the Wolstenholme Brothers, a few years later, who had their first studio in the 'orchard' of Boardman Lane. They also became famous Blackpool photographers. Abel Wolstenholme left an amazing legacy of photographs, mainly of Rhodes, and some of his glass negatives, which have recently been donated to the Old Grammar school Trust, are used here. Thomas Baddeley travelled extensively in the North West, seemingly for the love of capturing a scene that he knew would disappear all too soon. Like the Jackson and Wolstenholme Brothers, he obtained excellent results with his glass negatives. N.S. Roberts of Rochdale took many very good aerial views, and Entwistle Thorpe & Co. Ltd, founded 102 years ago and still in business, made a significant contribution, being commissioned by Middleton Council, mainly in connection with Compulsory Purchase Orders (CPOs). The *Middleton Guardian* has also had an important input with their high quality photographs.

Other photographers like Francis Frith, who founded the picture postcard firm, rose to fame nationally. He commissioned work from Roger Fenton, of the well-known Heywood family, who achieved national acclaim as a photographer himself from the 1850s. Some of the photographs are comparatively recent, as Middleton developed faster than any other town in the country between 1911 and 1971. Lawrence Kaye left an amazing legacy of photographs of streets and everyday scenes of the 1960s, '70s and '80s, which forms a large portion of the Middleton Library collection. Some are reproduced here with his blessing.

As late as 1770 Middleton was little more than a village, with barely twenty houses and was quite separate from Tonge and Alkrington. The origins of St Leonard's church are thought to date back to Saxon times and Middleton retained its typical Saxon structure of church, manor house, water powered corn mill, tithe barn and farm, all within close proximity, much longer than most surrounding towns. The church was on the hill, while the other buildings were by the river Irk below. Middleton Hall, where the Lords of the Manor of Middleton lived, had a moat and drawbridges in the early days. The Lords had close links with St Leonard's and held the patronage. There were thatched cottages along the road from Manchester to Rochdale (part of the Great Highway from Chester to York), by the church and in some folds.

Middleton folk used to have a rural, self-contained lifestyle, with small plots of land by their cottages, where they kept a cow or two and a pig and grew fruit and vegetables. Many would make their own butter and cheese, bake bread, bottle fruit, draw water from a nearby well, obtain coal locally and often not venture far from their hamlet. Some worked at their handlooms and were known by nicknames, such as Betty o' Booths.

It was during the Industrial Revolution that Middleton, along with most other towns, began to change, the population increasing as people came in from more rural areas to work in silk weaving, cotton mills, bleach and dye works and associated trades. By 1790 there were between four and five hundred people. Lord Suffield (Harbord Harbord) had succeeded the Asshetons by marriage in 1765 and started to lease land for development soon afterwards. In 1791 the town took a major step forward when he obtained the Market Charter at his own expense, authorising a market to be held in Middleton on Fridays and public fairs three times a year. He built a stone Market House and Shambles on the Long Street side of the Hall, with the Masons' Arms, built around the same time, between them. Basic necessities, such as corn, grain, flour, fruit, vegetables and cheese could then be bought locally from the stalls in the Market House. Cattle were traded and butchers' meat purchased from the Shambles, the area becoming known as Market Place. Prior to this, St Leonard's Square had been an earlier form of market place, with fairs and rush bearing festivals also being associated with the church.

The Top o' Middleton was the first area of the town to become well developed, with an early form of co-operative enabling some handloom silk weavers to build their own homes. Lord Suffield also leased land in Rhodes and Parkfield from the 1770s. Most of the centre of the town remained undeveloped however, being occupied by Middleton Hall and its extensive grounds.

Lord Suffield had his home on his estate in Norfolk and major change came when Middleton Hall was demolished in 1845, the estate was sold in 1848 and the Market House and Shambles were taken down in 1851. Tonge was still separate from Middleton at this time, being in Prestwich-cum-Oldham and it was already well developed. Between 1800 and 1850 the joint population of Middleton and Tonge had trebled, most of the population being handloom weavers of silk. The former Middleton Hall site became the scene of rapid development, with plans for Middleton Gas Works underway by 1846 and Thomas Dronsfield building two large cotton factories in 1851. The development of Market Place, Old Hall Street and the surrounding area followed soon afterwards.

Sir Samuel Morton Peto and Edward Lane Betts, the well-known railway contractors, were the purchasers of the Middleton Estate but they had to sell it in 1861. The Nuisance Removal Board appear to have seen the time of change as an opportunity to broaden their role, becoming Improvement Commissioners that year. They immediately obtained 'The Improvement Act for paving, draining, lighting, cleansing and otherwise improving', with administrative powers over both Middleton and Tonge, taking over the old Gas Company. Thomas Dronsfield, who built the Old Hall Mills, became a Commissioner. The mills, employing nearly 300 people, were burnt down in 1870. Such was the blaze, Manchester, Denton and Bury mobilised their fire engines, under the impression that the fire was in their area and hundreds of Oldham folk made their way to Platt's Mill, expecting to see it on fire. 'Old Cataract', the Commissioners' fire engine, was away for repair, and neither the jets from the temporary replacement nor the Hopwood engine could reach up to the site of the blaze, on the fifth storey of the mill. Somewhat surprisingly, the *Middleton Albion* of 22 December 1883 reported that Thomas Dronsfield had died in Strangeways Prison, after being convicted of trying to burn down his Old Hall Mills. Albert Booth of Rhodes House laid the foundation stone of the Albany Mill on their site in 1882 and it became a prominent landmark until its demolition in 1975.

The Industrial Revolution also brought the canal and railways and as opportunities for trade and travel increased life began to change…

One

Market Place

After the Market House and Shambles were demolished in 1851, John Rushton, a Wesleyan Methodist, and Henry Whalley, a promoter of the Albany Mill, built a row of properties on the former site of the Shambles. Market Place soon became the hub of the fast developing town, being home to at least five inns and a variety of shops, whose owners lived on the premises in the early years. It was also host to many events, such as wartime victory celebrations and election addresses, in addition to the market and fairs, with shopkeepers, such as Whitworths the newsagents, often placing stalls at the edges of the fairs. Market trading used to be from 2-8p.m. on Fridays, with the Market Bell being rung at 8p.m. sharp. The south-east side of Market Place was widened in 1938 to ease traffic congestion, causing the number of market stalls to be reduced from seventy-seven to fifty-one. Some stallholders came from as far a field as Garstang, Preston and Ramsbottom. The market moved to a larger site in Fountain Street in 1939, where it thrived until November 1972, when it was transferred to Chapel Street, at the bottom of Wood Street, so that the Civic Hall could be built. 1972 was also the year when businesses in Market Place, including Broadbent's, Percival's and the Masons' Arms, had to close, prior to the construction of the new roundabout and Assheton Way. The latter two effectively cut off the north end of Long Street from today's town centre.

Sam Stansfield, who succeeded his father in a clothing and furnishing business at No. 38, was one of Market Place's most colourful characters. His half-crown screwed to the counter, which every youth attempted to pocket, and his renowned advertisements in the *Guardian* are well remembered: 'Ladies beware, Sam's trousers are down again, 3/9d a leg, all seats free!' 'You've never felt felt till you've felt the felt in one of Sam's felt caps'. 'If th'hat doesn't fit, Mrs, then t'box will'. Sam died in 1941.

Middleton Hall, home of the Lords of the Manor. It was demolished in 1845, having been largely rebuilt in 1805. This sketch was drawn from memory in 1887 by Walter Acton, using measurements taken by Absalom Wellens (born 1815), a former agent for the Middleton Hall Estate.

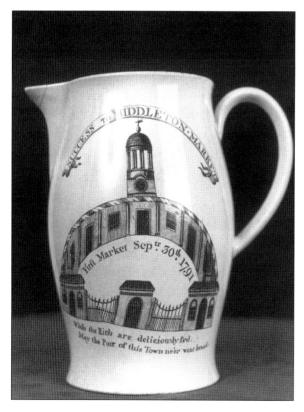

A Staffordshire pottery jug portraying the Market House, that stood close to Middleton Hall. Lord Suffield had several jugs made to commemorate his obtaining the Market Charter on 23 June 1791. Some jugs were smaller, others had views of the Hall. Examples can be seen at Middleton Library.

10

The Assheton Arms, Market Place, *c.* 1880. To the left is Police Constable Stepney of Wood Street and Moses Aspinall, an auctioneer, who used to live at the premises to the right of the inn. Robert Steeple is on the right. The coachmen are John Pickles, Edward Blomeley and E. Bowyer.

Market Place, 1904. The Williams Deacons and Manchester and Salford Bank (later Union, see also page 114), designed by Edgar Wood, replaced Moses Aspinall's property. On the left of the Assheton Arms are new stables (white door) with a function room above.

Turner's Garretts, Long Street. Thomas Turner the tailor, the Jacksons and Edgar Wood once had premises here. Following demolition, Lord Derby opened Middleton's third post office on the site in 1905. To the left is the Manchester and County Bank, designed by Edgar Wood. On the opposite corner of Sadler Street is John Steeple's shop, established in 1859.

Steeple's ironmongers shop in 1975. After over a century of business the hardware and method of display seem little changed! In the doorway is the proprietor, Eric Whitworth, who died in 1977. Steeples had also been mill furnishers and butchers and had a music shop at the bottom of Wood Street.

Long Street, c. 1880. Salem Chapel is in the centre distance, in what later became Central Gardens. The Central Co-op Stores and Hall (complete with clock, see page 118) were opened in 1871. Premises to its left, including Stansfield's pawnbroker's, were demolished in the 1930s, to make way for additional Co-op premises. The Masons' Arms is on the left.

Celebrating the Coronation of King Edward VII, Market Place, 1902. Notice the soldiers on the left firing a gun salute (or are they shooting pigeons on top of the Albany?) The Shuttle Inn is in the middle of the row of property. Its small back yard was used for Middleton Brass Band practices until the inn's closure in 1907.

Market Place was an excellent vantage point for watching processions pass by, especially at Whitsuntide or Anniversary time. This huge walk was from the parish church around 1910.

King George V, Queen Mary and the Duke of York are in the stand at the corner of Corporation Street. The child at the window of the Market Inn is Lena Fletcher (later Thornton), who was visiting her grandparents, Ruth and Joseph Chadwick, landlords of the inn.

Providence school being used as a hospital for wounded soldiers during the First World War. Standing centre back is Agnes Livingstone, a grocer and florist in Rhodes. Local Girl Guides endowed a bed and distributed fruit, sweets and cakes to the soldiers.

Providence Independent chapel (left) opened in 1859. The school was built in 1850, as the former chapel. Previously, the congregation had met in various locations including Turner's Garretts. The chapel of 1859 has been empty since 1991, when the congregation joined Alkrington URC and the school was demolished.

Few will remember the Board of Trade Labour Exchange in Lodge Street, seen here with the Parish Church Anniversary Walk, passing by. The building is now a gardening and DIY shop. At one time there was a Pinfold for stray animals nearby, where the road from Market Place turned right towards Oldham.

Inside the Labour Exchange. The décor is Spartan but any offers of help would have been invaluable, especially in the depression of the 1930s. According to a contemporary visiting card Miss Devine was the manager and her telephone number was '108 Middleton'.

September 1939, and with the outbreak of war Market Place is excavated for air-raid shelters. No one seems concerned by the plume of black smoke behind the new Co-op stores! The new gas showrooms and Burton's Tailors are to the left.

Wartime precautions continue in Market Place as the Union Bank (now Royal Bank of Scotland) and the adjacent police station are sandbagged against air raids. Lodge Street is in the distance, on the right.

The Market Inn closed in 1930 and Fred Broadbent and his wife Vinnie (*née* Cumberledge) took just fourteen shillings during their first week in its former premises, where they opened a ladies' fashion shop. The air-raid shelter entrances remained until 1948, when the gardens were created. The shelters themselves were forgotten until 1974, when workman excavating for the new underpass and roundabout found them intact.

Bob's Stores, No. 32 Market Place. Rationing on certain products continued well into the 1950s, with tea still rationed to half a pound per month. Ernest Ackroyd and Mrs Nuttall are on the left with Doris Kerfoot on the right.

Shops in Market Place, *c.* 1960, when Cyril Bernstein's occupied the Albany Mill. Corporation Street is on the right. The shops were demolished in 1972 to make way for the roundabout and Assheton Way.

The Broadbents also opened children's and menswear departments lower down Market Place. The UCP (see page 20) was across Mason Street. Prior to this it was in 'White City' (see page 29). Among other things it sold tripe and 'duck 'n muffins', otherwise known as 'savvy ducks'.

Mayor's Sunday, May 1963, and the procession heads for the annual service at the parish church. Councillor Olive Taylor (Mayor), Edith Wellens (Deputy Mayor) and Frank Johnson (Town Clerk) are preceded by Aldermen Emerson and Heywood and the mace-bearer, Norman Bolton. Directly behind the mayor are Councillor Sid Chisholm (wearing a trilby) and Harry Hind with Chief Superintendent Alf Baron.

The centre of Middleton in 1948, Market Place being the upper of the two triangles, with the former site of Middleton Hall to its right, now heavily developed. However, the distinctive curve of Fountain Street still follows the course of the millrace that ran from a sluice near Townley Street, past the Hall gardens to serve the corn mill in Mill Street. The Victory Cinema in Wood Street and the Co-op Hall, Long Street, can also be seen. The lower triangle is of course Central Gardens, featured in the next section.

Opposite: Passing through Market Place and seeing the beautifully decorated Christmas tree went a long way to getting Christmas off to a good start, even if it was raining. Middletonians gathered around the tree each year to sing carols and, unlike today, neither the tree nor the crib in the lower corner of Market Place was ever vandalised!

When the Market Place shops were demolished in 1972, much of the area became temporarily derelict, awaiting work on the new roundabout and Assheton Way, which started in 1974.

The newly constructed roundabout and Assheton Way, as seen from the top of the gasholder, c. 1976. Try to imagine how things were; Middleton Hall and its south facing gardens, the bustling markets and Wakes fairs, the celebrations and processions or more recently the Market Place shops and well-manicured gardens.

Two

Around
Central Gardens

The site of Central Gardens was formerly the mill meadow and the bottom end of the dam serving the corn mill of Middleton Hall. Like Market Place, it has seen many changes. The triangular shape was formed after the Castleton and Great Heaton Land Act of 1804 authorised the building of Manchester New Road, which met Manchester Old Road just south of the Market House. The Gem Cinema, on the site of the former corn mill, was demolished in 1920. It was not until the late 1920s that the corporation decided to buy up property and create the Central Gardens. Soon after the aerial view on the next page was taken, Salem Chapel, the tram office and other buildings were demolished.

The Mayor, Alderman J. Cockshott, opened the Central Gardens in October 1934. With their fountain and colourful flower displays they were considered beautiful enough to attract people to visit Middleton from districts as far afield as Ancoats and Collyhurst as part of a day out! When the gardens were dug up in the 1980s, the foundations of the old corn mill were re-discovered. The fountain, a feature for more than fifty years, was broken up and dropped into the underground toilets. The whole area was then covered with modern brick paving. However, just over twenty years later, the area was redesigned and a modern fountain installed, when it was renamed Middleton Gardens.

The junction of Manchester Old and New Roads, August 1925. Mill Dam Side (later Fountain Street) has the mill-race still running down one side of it. Middleton Liberal Club's bowling green became the site of the Baths and Market. T.B. Wood's Park Mill Lodge was later drained and it is now a car park. The river Irk can be seen entering Jackie Booth's Field to be rejoined by the mill-race flowing from under Mather & Ormesher's Mill (see also page 36).

Looking back up Long Street at the time of Queen Victoria's Golden Jubilee, 22 June 1897, when celebrations took place in the bunting strewn streets. The ice-cream shop at the bottom of Wood Street must have done a roaring trade on what was evidently a hot summer's day.

A similar view to above with Edgar Wood's famous shelter, drinking fountain and horse-trough, donated to the town by his stepmother to commemorate the Golden Jubilee. To enable road widening it was moved to Queen Street, near to the junction of Oldham Road, in 1925, and was finally demolished in 1960.

Long Street, with Lawson's confectioner's shop (see below) standing at the corner of Old Hall Street, c. 1956. A bank has replaced the ice-cream shop and the 'modern cars and buses' render it unsafe to pass the time of day in the middle of Long Street! Maurice Hamer, whose father, Charles, owned Radio Relay, is driving the BSA sports car.

Henry Whalley Lawson's confectioners and wine and spirit merchant's shop, Nos 2–4 Long Street. Emily Travis (later Duckett) is in the doorway of the shop where she worked with her sisters Mary and Annie. Ada Allman worked in the bake-house. The business was later taken over by Ernest McDougall.

Woolworth's stores, Long Street, 10 February 1971. The Mayor, Councillor Geoffrey Allen, shares a smile with staff and customer a few days before 'D Day', when decimalisation was introduced and we said goodbye to pounds, shillings and pence.

Long Street, 1962, with Old Hall Street to the right. Prior to the Arndale Centre being built this was a thriving shopping area with Lawson's, Timpson's and Freeman, Hardy and Willis being some of its well-known names.

Old Hall Street during the flood of 1927. By the late 1850s it was housing no less than five beer houses or inns. The clock on the left is outside John Tommy Kay's watch and clock makers shop at No. 21.

A Calvary Hall procession in Old Hall Street. Mrs Evelyn Jenyons, whose father was Charles Dennis (see page 30), is on the left. Calvary Hall, later named the church of the Nazarene, was above S. Wellens & Sons' garage in Old Hall Street.

Cooper & Jagger's, No. 4 Old Hall Street, 1909. Edward Smith (father of Margaret Smith, the local historian) is on the left. Some orders received by postcard were marked 'Mr Smith to cut the bacon'. Orders were delivered by pony and trap (including the weekly order for Hopwood Hall) or by handcart in the town centre.

Manchester Old Road, looking north from the Dusty Miller across the site that later became Central Gardens, c. 1928. To the right of Salem Chapel are the three shops designed by Edgar Wood in 1908 and known as 'White City'. They incorporated a reinforced concrete roof and green and white tiling, his first use of colour in external architecture.

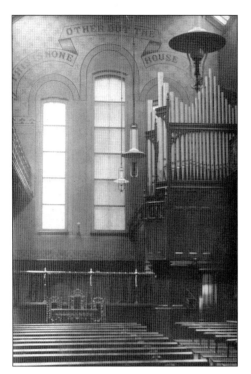

Salem Chapel, complete with gaslights. When it was demolished in 1928, its congregation moved to the newly built Alkrington Congregational church, taking the table, chairs and organ with them. As with many churches of the time, Salem had its own football team and three members of the Ashton family played for it.

The Dusty Miller. It was built opposite the corn mill and Mill Lane, *c.* 1772. The landlord, James H. Roberts, is in the doorway with 'Black Charley' in front of him. He was Charles Dennis of Wood Street, who was born in Virginia where he and his mother were sold into slavery. He was the first black person to live in Middleton and he died here in 1939.

Billy Partington fills up one of S. Wellens & Sons' cars in the 1920s, prior to going 'on a wedding'. The roadside petrol pump is on Manchester Old Road, outside what is now MacDonalds. James Parkinson, who had a farm on Sandy Lane, was the owner of the butcher's shop opposite, next door to Smith's milliners shop (see also page 29).

The Dusty Miller is on the right. Construction work for the Arndale Centre, that so radically changed the town centre of Middleton, can be seen in the background. The Duchess of Kent opened the centre in March 1972.

Central Gardens (nicknamed Pea Gardens, after the underground public conveniences), as seen from the Lever's Arms, which had to close in 1971. The Palace Arcade can be seen to the left of the Old Roebuck. Formerly a wood yard, it housed several shops including Clarkson's the butchers, Barsh's tailors and Towler's toffees.

Central Gardens looking south, with Morton's well-known grocers and florist's shop (see opposite) at the top.

Morton's shop at No. 29, Manchester New Road. They moved here from their former premises in Oldham Road (see page 42) around 1900.

Inside Morton's during the mid-1950s. Len Morton later sold the green fruit department to the Middleton & Tonge Co-op but continued with floristry in the shop extension until retirement.

Middleton and Tonge Public Baths, Manchester Old Road (near Lime Street) opened in 1864. The plain concrete tank and lack of filtration plants did not deter the eager youngsters, who had to have a scrub down and cold shower first. Even so it became obvious when the twice-weekly change of water was due!

Frank Watson, an attendant at the old baths mentioned above. He was reputed to be able to swim at least two lengths under water (the pool was twenty yards long). After the death of Mr Martin Carter he became superintendent at the Fountain Street Baths (opposite), which replaced them.

The Fountain Street Baths opened 27 October 1938. The pools were drained in the autumn and covered with dance floors, becoming the Baths Ballroom until April. Glen Gray and his band were the resident orchestra, playing for capacity crowds at the Friday and Saturday night dances.

A Whitsuntide gathering in Fountain Street, seen from the balcony of the baths in 1953. The banners from left to right are those from the Sunday schools of St Stephens, Temple Street Baptist and Calvary Hall. The baths, along with the sports hall and civic hall may well disappear soon if a proposed supermarket is built.

The old Town Hall, Gas Street (later Corporation Street). It was opened in 1861 as the Middleton and Tonge Improvement Commissioner's headquarters, becoming the Town Hall when borough status was gained in 1886. In 1925 the mill-race was culverted, Fountain Street widened and the Town Hall moved to the newly acquired Parkfield House.

Mather, Ormesher & Co. Ltd, dyers and polishers of cotton yarns for braids, electrical wire covering and other goods. They were at Bridge Mills, near Jackie Booth's Field (see also page 24).

The Central Working Men's Club, which was reached through a ginnel off Booth Street, in the Jackie Booth's Field area. Some Wakes celebrations were held in Jackie Booth's Field for at least eighty years prior to the fairs moving here in 1939, with foot, pony and whippet races being held on Wakes Monday.

The 6th Lancashire Fusiliers, A & E Companies, parading down Manchester New Road outside the Drill Hall, as seen from the Commercial Hotel, 5 August 1914. A large crowd, no doubt including some wives and families, look on somewhat anxiously.

Jackie Booth's Field, 1968, with Mrs Margaret Jessop standing on a footbridge over the Irk. Marsh Row is on the right. It was near this bridge that the mill-race rejoined the Irk. The river was culverted in 1969, prior to the new road system and bus station being built.

Marsh Row, with Manchester New Road and the Warwick Mill (left) and Irk Mill chimneys at the top. This area was prone to flooding, with water reaching first floor level of many houses in 1927, leaving tidemarks on bedroom furniture. These former silk weavers' houses were demolished in 1960.

Three
Tonge and Alkrington

Tonge took its name from the shape of its land, resembling a 'tongue' between the river Irk and Wince Brook. It was in Prestwich-cum-Oldham, being south of the Irk, which formed the boundary with Middleton. Within living memory there were Tonge folk who never went into Middleton, as they considered it quite separate. The Tonge Hall Estate covered 160 acres, 100 of them moorland. Its Hall has survived partly because it is situated above the road to Oldham. In 1780 there were only seventy-four people in Tonge but the area experienced the most rapid growth of any locally, and by 1850 the Little Park and Lark Hill areas were well developed. Little Park was formerly a private park between Middleton Hall and the Irk, but the name spread to new development south of the Irk. It housed many of the people who had come in from the villages to work as silk weavers or at the dye works and it was also home to the first local Co-op shop. Nearby Lark Hill, with its neat rows of terraced houses and communal backyards, was mainly occupied by cotton operatives.

The Alkrington Hall Estate covered over 700 acres, with many twenty to thirty acre farms on the moss. Alkrington became part of Middleton in 1879. It remained largely agricultural until the building of the Alkrington Garden Village in the 1930s and further development in the late 1960s. Only Ramsden Farm survives, having been farmed by the Partingtons for over seventy years, but following the death of George Partington in 2001, its agricultural future is uncertain.

Hardly a blade of grass is left in the Tonge side of Little Park, as seen from the gasholder in the early 1940s. The Warwick Mill is on the extreme left, followed by the Irk Mill and Tonge Mill, which is at the junction of Oldham Road and Manchester New Road, opposite the Drill Hall. The more rural areas of Alkrington Wood, Rhodes Lodges and the water tower at Blackley are in the distance, behind Manchester New Road (formerly Lever Brow). The clarity of the photograph is typical of those taken by Entwistle Thorpe.

Simpson Court, showing the rear view of Nos 16-24 Simpson Street, whose windows have been 'modernised', *c.* 1920. The communal yard and shared privies were features of many handloom weavers' cottages built in the early nineteenth century. On the right are Nos 1-5 Oldham Road with the Irk and Warwick Mills behind.

Boats from the lakes at Heaton Park and Boggart Hole Clough were brought on the back of lorries belonging to Whitefield Velvet Company, Parkfield, to help rescue people trapped in their homes during the Middleton Flood of 1927. Harry Healey stands by his boat in Simpson Street with Park Street to the right.

Henry Thomas Morton's greengrocer0s shop, Oldham Road, (opposite the Warwick Mill). The business later moved to Manchester New Road (see page 33), where Henry's son, Leonard, eventually took over.

The 'Banana King' float, a second prize winner, is seen near Morton's garage in Old Hall Street. From left to right are Fred Haworth, Len Morton (1903-1975), Henry Morton (died 1940s) and Charley Middleton (right of the cab), who was engineer at Tonge Dyeing Company and also repaired model galleons for the Parker Gallery, London.

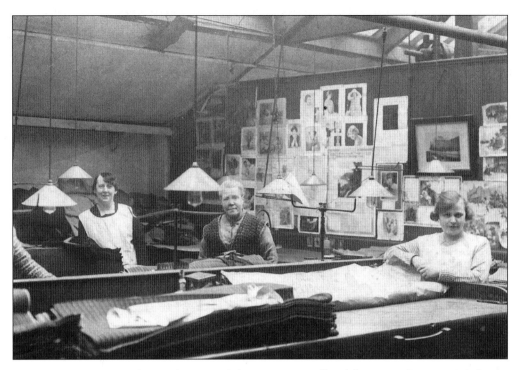

Parker Lords & Co. Ltd, Winders & Polishers, Tonge Mill, Oldham Road, 1920. On the far right of the cut room, where weavers took their material to be checked over, is Lena Hellon (*née* Clapham). She was a winder and Mrs Brierley is next to her. Richard J. Parker and Abraham Lord JP established the firm in 1865.

Surrage's shop, No. 250 Oldham Road. The shop appears to be selling sweets but later, Harold Surrage and his sister Carrie (pictured) sold hardware. Harold retired in the late 1960s. With careful examination, houses on the opposite side of Oldham Road can be seen reflected in the window.

A bird's eye view of Lark Hill, *c.* 1940. Photographers soon found that the top of the new waterless gasholder was an excellent viewpoint. It was built into a tight slot between the Irk and Park Lane, close to three existing gasholders. Oldham Road runs down the centre with Middleton Station, the railway embankment, St Michaels and St Peter's churches and the mills on Grimshaw Lane and Oldham Road clearly visible. The EWS (emergency water supply) sign at the corner of Taylor Street points towards Wince Brook, several hundred yards away, yet the Irk is much closer under the trees to the left!

Opposite: Ken Mingham (left) and Stan Robinson on top of the new gasholder, inaugurated 18 September 1935, its height being 163ft to where the men are standing. In 1987 demolition had to be delayed because kestrels were found to be nesting at the top.

Looking from Manchester New Road towards Warwick Mill, 1936. The Walker family, who were also butchers and helped to establish the town's first Co-op shop, opened therein the Jolly Butcher, opposite the shop in 1818. The Jolly Butcher was demolished in 1952.

St Peter's Catholic church, Taylor Street. The original building of 1867 was demolished in 1910 and the present church opened a year later. Prior to 1867, mass was celebrated above a shop in Old Hall Street.

A St Peter's procession, Oldham Road, 1950. The wet day has not deterred the May Queen, Mary Stone, or her attendants who include Terry Connor, Michael Sullivan and Terry Davey. Tonge Mill is behind.

Albert Street, built in the 1840s. The Warwick Mill, extreme left, was built for cotton spinning in 1907. Now with listed building status it should remain with us as an example of Middleton's many mills. The houses, which had been refaced and had communal backyards, had no such security and were demolished in the 1960s.

Middleton Station, opened in 1857 and closed in 1964. The land between St Michael's church and Tonge Hall was excavated to allow the station and its sidings to be built. One abandoned plan was for a station to be in the Higher Wood Street area (where Peto Street now marks the intended spot), with the line ultimately going through to Bury.

St Michael's churchyard, with Grimshaw Lane and Kirkway behind. Grundy's Memorial Masons' crane was used to lower a memorial stone in place, to be dedicated by the vicar, the Revd H.W.N. Cave, who is also on the next photograph. Grundys had a long connection with the church and they later built the tower.

Members of St Michael's church have assembled on the vicarage lawn prior to their annual walk. The bandsmen are about to play, girls carry garlands, parents watch proudly and the Church Lads' Brigade stand by their carbines.

Revd Harry Evans, Rural Dean of Middleton, near St Michael's church, where he ministered for over thirty years. The 'Waterloo' church of 1839, serving Tonge-cum-Alkrington, was enlarged in 1902, with the side-chapel being added in 1926 and the tower in 1930. Waterloo churches were built with government money in areas experiencing rapid growth.

Lark Hill, as seen from St Michael's tower, 1972, with little surviving after the CPOs, apart from St Peter's church, Gilmour Street, the Warwick and Irk Mills, and the gasholder. The newly-opened Arndale Centre is in the middle and Rhodes Chimney in the background. The Irk Mill was demolished two years later.

An unusual view of the mills of Middleton, looking over much of the area seen on the aerial view of page 40. The Drill Hall and Tonge Dye Works are in the foreground with the Tonge, Irk and Warwick Mills to the right.

Townley Street, with the Oldham corporation tram operating the No. 3 route, caught up in the procession at the junction with Oldham Road, c. 1924. The route was the last survivor in Middleton, ceasing on 11 June 1934. The Railway Hotel, built 1857, is on the right. The incinerator chimney and that of Albany Mill are behind.

James and Sarah Marshall and family outside their beautiful cottage in Springvale, *c.* 1895. Arthur was born in 1888 and Emily in 1890.

The junction of Springvale and Townley Street, September 1937, with the Albany Mill behind. Prior to Princes Bridge being built, the river Irk was forded at this point. W.H. James & Co., publishers of *The Advertiser*, occupied the property at the junction prior to demolition, when they moved across the road to their newly-built print works.

A Tonge loomhouse built in 1768, at No. 1 Off Kenyon Lane. The original mullioned windows can be seen. Middleton favoured 'Yorkshire lights' (see page 74), where the middle window pane could be moved behind one of the two outer ones, presumably giving better ventilation for the silk weaving. Mrs Alice Clegg (*née* Collinge) is on the left and Cary Tonge is to the right.

Tonge Hall, dating back to 1590. Over the centuries the Hall has been considerably altered and its restoration still continues. Henry Tonge was the earliest recorded inhabitant of a hall here in 1313. He had fifty acres of 'land', six acres of meadow, four acres of wood and one hundred acres of moor.

Booth's grocery and provisions shop and post office, and Allen Marcroft's shop, at the corner of Oldham Road and Don Street, 1959. The Hillman Minx belonged to one of the directors of Vitafoam.

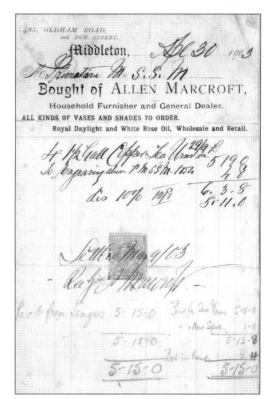

An original invoice for goods from Allen Marcroft's shop, dated 30 April 1903. Shops were often positioned near the mills to catch passing trade.

British Vita, formerly Vitafoam, was one of Middleton's largest employers. This view from the Rex Mill shows the Don Mill, which they purchased in 1955, on the left just after the fire of 5 August 1961. This was built as a cotton mill in 1899-1900. On the right are Soudan Mills Nos 1 and 2. (Reproduced courtesy of British Vita Plc).

The Rex Mill, c. 1902. Ina Ansell (front middle), Edmund Arnfield (left) and others are working the three pairs of mules in the basement. It was lit by gas, which could be a hazard, as fluff from the cotton often floated up to the lights and ignited. After closure as a cotton mill in 1955, the Rex became the home of Senior Service Cigarettes from 1959-1986.

After three days of torrential rain the raging river Irk burst its banks, breaching the canal embankment at the side of the aqueduct at Mills Hill on 27 July 1927. As a result millions of gallons of water emptied into the already swollen river. The photograph is taken from the canal with Middleton to the left looking towards 'Top Drum' (The Gardeners' Arms).

Mills Hill, 1935. The Malta Mill, built in 1905, and the Rochdale Canal are in the foreground. Opposite are the Co-operative Wholesale Society (CWS) Preserve Works and Vinegar Brewery with the railway line behind. By 1916, the CWS were producing 15,000 tons of jam and marmalade each year, bringing seventy wagon loads of fruit a day by rail from their own farms in high season. The Jam Works Shunter actually hauled the trucks inside the works. Baytree Lane passes under the railway line. Notice the terraced houses, purposely built close to the mills to accommodate the workers, leaving little excuse for being late for the 6a.m. shift! Oldham Road and the Don, Rex and Soudan Mills are in the distance, at the top.

Lowbands, Jumbo, 1860, a scene of major significance, as an early co-operative was started here, which ultimately led to the founding of the CWS. Wince Brook is on the left, a well in the foreground and Middleton Church in the background.

The CWS Preserve, Marmalade & Peel Works (opened 1897). Along with the Vinegar Brewery, Pickle & Sauce Works (opened 1909) they stretched almost the entire length of Mills Hill Road. They closed in 1968.

Wrapping Christmas Puddings at the CWS Preserve Works, Mills Hill Road. Many Middleton and Chadderton folk worked here, with six hundred, swelling to over a thousand in high season, employed on jam production alone.

Bradshaw Hall, photographed by the Jackson Brothers, who used to wash their photographic plates and prints in its well. When the Earls of Derby owned the estate, a branch of the Chadderton family occupied the Hall. There was a fold of cottages with flag walls, a farm, a pit and a corn mill, which was later used for weaving. The estate covered much of the Grimshaw Lane area.

The Middleton Junction Wesleyan Methodist chapel, opened on 28 April 1891. It stood on the corner of Grimshaw Lane and Potts Street, with the school around the corner in Lees Street, opposite the Greengate Brewery. The Burton family of Rhodes Works were among the founders of the first fellowship here in the early 1800s.

The Wesleyan's annual procession passing Middleton Junction Station, Green Lane (see also opposite), 4 June 1921. Frank Crompton (with the coat over his arm) and George Simpson are leading the men.

Middleton's first station was at Mills Hill in 1839, then a new one was built down the line at Jumbo when a branch to Oldham was added in 1842. Originally known as Oldham Junction, it became 'Middleton' later that year. A decade later it was renamed Middleton Junction and the name was also adopted for the area. The station closed in 1964; then, in 1985, it re-opened at Mills Hill. Confusing, isn't it?

A steam train on the Middleton branch line, with the roof of St Gabriel's church and houses on Greenhill Road and Aspinall Street behind, c. 1930. A footbridge crossed the railway from Pine Street (formerly Rough Lane) to Aspinall Street.

A sign on the station platform warns drivers of a 4mph speed limit. This notice perhaps came about after an out-of-control train failed to stop and ended up in a work's yard!

A tramcar stands at the Middleton Junction terminus on Grimshaw Lane, the boom already turned round for the return journey to Middleton. The Jackson Brothers once lived in the first house on the left, now No. 350. The shop has traded continuously as a chemist's from at least 1845. On the right is John Willie Lee's Brewery, founded in 1828.

A St Gabriel's church procession, passing the same point as opposite. The circular sign on the left states that it is one mile to Middleton, two and a half miles to Hollinwood, 195 miles to London and then reminds drivers 'Safety First'. This area was in the Bradshaw Hall Estate.

'The Seven Sisters', the Crabtree girls from Middleton Junction, who are opening the Gift Day at St Gabriel's church in 1959. They are left to right, Dolly, Florence, Ada, Emma, Jessie, Alice and Clara.

Alkrington, with Manchester New Road and Alkrington Green in the foreground and Mount Road and Kingsway going off to the right, 1921. Mount Road passes Lancashire Fold on its left, as it winds its way up to The Mount (see also page 65), seen here surrounded by trees. Like Bradshaw Fold, the cottages, farm, well and coal pit of Lancashire Fold were clustered together, dating back to the seventeenth century, when the Enclosure of Land Act brought former field workers together. Spa Cottage overlooks Stocks and Bank Top, on the path to Ashton Lane, on what is now Kirkway. To the right of Lancashire Fold is the old Wagon Road (tramway) used to transport coal across the fields (through what is now the Welsh Estate) to the washpits, railway and canal. Alkrington Colliery, complete with its twin subterranean canals, closed in 1897. Sunk Lane can be seen wending its way from the fold towards Sandy Lane via Ramsden, Roundthorn and Hard Meadow Farms.

Wince Brook Cottages, with Ashton Lane beyond. The bridge over Wince Brook is just out of sight between the two sets of houses.

The Mount, formerly the colliery manager's residence, stood on the prominence overlooking the top end of Mount Road. There was a local legend that however foggy it was on The Moss, the plantation and area around The Mount was always clear.

Stocks Cottages, Alkrington, 1936. Old Pendlebury, a famous botanist and gardener, lived at the cottage on the left. About twenty silk weavers formed an early co-operative next door at the home of William Taylor. Thomas Brierley, famous for his 'Countrified Pieces' had handlooms in the two cottages at the end of the row.

Spa Cottage, said to be haunted, seen from the south east in Tommy Griffin's time, April 1937. To the left of the front door is Spa Well, noted for its crystal clear water with supposed medicinal properties and never known to fail. This was a very old settlement with records going back beyond 1212.

Moss Farm, Alkrington, August 1937, photographed by Thomas Baddeley when Milton Schofield lived here. A boy is fishing in one of two ponds, known by their shape as the 'Apple and Pear'. The tower on the skyline is that of Moston Mill. Alkrington Moss school is now built on this site.

Building Mainway. Just how rural Alkrington was before the Second World War can be seen here, one misty morning. It was originally intended to build Mainway to Greengate and Kirkway to Victoria Avenue East. The first houses were built in the late 1930s.

An Alkrington Garden Village advertisement, 1936. The garden cities were a revolution in house building, with easy rates enabling ordinary people to buy from a wide variety of houses, all having a garden. The Alkrington development was described as 'the largest garden city outside Letchworth'.

Alkrington Hall, built in 1723 by the Ashton Lever family, on the site of an earlier Hall. Its 700-acre estate included much of the land seen on the aerial view on page 64, such as Lancashire Fold. Middleton Council purchased the Hall and some of the land in 1942.

Four

Rhodes to Kid Clough

Rhodes' people were noted for their clannishness, longevity, poetry and music, with only three main families in the early days. The village began to develop when Daniel Burton, a bleacher, transferred his business from Manchester to Rhodes in 1784, leasing land from Sir Harbord Harbord. As business increased, the Burtons moved their printing department to a mill on Wood Street. Being among the first to use power looms, they risked rioting from those who feared that the new technology would rob people of jobs. The Burtons were Wesleyan Methodists, with two of Daniel's sons, Charles and James, being ministers; a third, John, founding the Rhodes Wesleyan chapel and a fourth, George, being a local preacher. After a riot at their Rhodes Works, George was preaching at the Manchester Old Road chapel, when on announcing his text as 'What can I do to be saved?', a shrill voice responded immediately with 'Send for the Scots Greys!' They were the cavalry troop sent from Manchester to quell the recent riot and to the Luddite Riot at their Wood Street Mill in 1812. In spite of tragic consequences at the latter (see page 82) the firm prospered until 1833, when the Rhodes premises were leased to Salis Schwabe & Co., who had a workforce of over a thousand by the 1850s. The Schwabe family became benefactors, providing a library, reading room, schools and other facilities in the village. The Chimney school was used as a forerunner of the drill hall and for other functions, such as the Drum and Fife Band rehearsals. Schwabes were themselves taken over by the Calico Printers Association (CPA) in 1899.

Canon Durnford of St Leonard's founded a daughter church, All Saints, in Rhodes and another, Holy Trinity, in Parkfield during his ministry. Lord Suffield had also leased land in Parkfield from the 1770s, mainly for silk weavers' cottages and for dye and print works.

An aerial view of Rhodes, 1939, with Rhodes Chimney towering over Manchester Old Road, as it runs northwards to Middleton. Rhodes (Schwabe's) Chimney was 321 feet high (with a further thirty-one feet below ground). John Ashton of Blackley built it in 1846, using one and a half million bricks, and within thirty-two weeks of the first brick being laid, smoke was coming out of the chimney. The boilers were in the works on the opposite side of the main road. The Rhodes Lodges, which served the works, cover a massive fourteen acres and are supplied by springs and dams on North Manchester Golf Club land. The clubhouse (Rhodes House) was formerly a home of the Burtons and later of Salis Schwabe. Road widening in 1936 resulted in the loss of part of two lodges and the demolition of the White Houses opposite them. During the Second World War, a bomb exploded on the edge of one lodge and a photograph of the damage clearly shows a pair of swans watching what is going on from a safe distance!

Rhodes Wood, when it was a pleasant area for country walks and children could play happily.

Rhodes Wood, with the attractive view looking towards Rhodes Chimney. Notice the Pump House between the lodges, used in exceptionally dry weather. The lodges used to be known locally as 'The Lake District' and Heywood Road as 'West End'.

Schwabe's fire brigade. Most large works had their own fire fighters and engines. Schwabe's had five fire engines, ranging from twelve horsepower to forty horsepower. Mr A. Kymer, Schwabe's chief engineer, was at one time captain of the brigade.

Looking south-east from the top of Rhodes Chimney, 1923, with the river Irk meandering towards Manchester and Boothroyden Road at the top. A similar view today would show the M60 motorway crossing the top of the photograph.

Boothroyden, *c.* 1908. The camera was a magnet for local children and their inclusion in the scene ensured that copies would sell well! Half way down the road is the bridge over the Irk with bleach works nearby. The Irk marks the boundary between Middleton and Manchester at this point.

A weaving shed, Factory Brow, Rhodes, *c.* 1896. Bob Thorpe is on the front row, second from left.

Boardman Lane, *c*. 1908. Abel Wolstenholme is finding many potential customers for a postcard, taken at the bottom end. Land for Boardman Lane was leased from Sir Harbord Harbord in 1786, mainly for handloom silk weavers' cottages.

Towards the top end of Boardman Lane, 1962, where time appears to have stood still for Nos 106-110. The lady is still wearing clogs and a long skirt and the houses have original Yorkshire lights and latches on baton doors, although one also has a Yale lock. Sadly, things were about to change with the clearance orders.

Delivering CWS flour in Peter Street (near Chapel Street), Rhodes. Flour was produced at the CWS Star Mill, Oldham, flannel at Littleborough, clothing at Leeds, biscuits at Crumpsall, tobacco in Manchester and so forth.

A police funeral at Rhodes Methodist church. The coffin is carried on a gun carriage and a policeman rides postillion on one of the horses. Both photographs on this page are by Abel Wolstenholme.

Thomas Hayes by the Barbers' Arms, Manchester Old Road. Three members of the Hayes family held the license between 1890 and 1927. Next door, to the left, is a smithy run by Joseph Boardman, followed by his son William. The Barbers' Arms was rebuilt in 1930.

The rear view of former silk weavers' cottages, Nos 47-53 Parkfield, *c.* 1960. Among the first in the area, they appear to have originally been built without back doors. Not everyone had a communal backyard!

Holy Trinity church, Parkfield, before the vestry extension. It was consecrated in 1862, being a daughter church of St Leonard's. The vicarage behind, with its numerous lofty rooms, is typical of the Victorian era. The new vicarage, acquired 110 years later, is more suited to today's modest stipend!

Holy Trinity opened a Mission Room on Higher Wood Street in 1884, close to the parochial boundary with St Leonard's. It was used for services, a Sunday school and small meetings, and as a focal point for processions to and from Parkfield, as seen here around 1900.

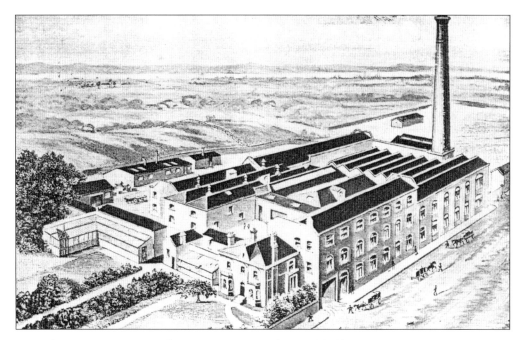

Samuel Lawton & Sons Mill, Cross Street Works, Parkfield, *c.* 1912. It specialised in the finishing, embossing and watering of silk, also working with plushes, velvets, satins and moirés. Parts of the mill dated back to around 1800. The manager's impressive house and garden can be seen on the left.

Some of Lawton's workforce. Notice they are all wearing clogs, hardwearing and useful for keeping feet warm on flag floors. Like Schwabe's, and many other works, they had their own fire brigade, as fires were common in mills.

Guests celebrate the Mayor Making of Councillor Jack Berry at Middleton Town Hall, Parkfield, originally the home of Daniel Burton. Guests here in 1960 include Mr and Mrs J.W. Johnson (owners of the garage in Corporation Street), Mr and Mrs A. Peirce, Mr and Mrs F. Hunt (of Hunt & Moscrop) and Mr Sam Taylor (Manager of the Co-op on Kingsway).

Woodside Terrace, Langley, 1951. It was on the left hand side of Demesne Street, now Wood Street, near to the present day shops at the junction with Windermere Road.

Demesne Street in the 1880s. It took its name from the Middleton Estate land on which it was built, and along with Top Street (on the left) linked Wood Street to estate farms such as Woodside, High Barn and Demesne, on what is now Langley. The path then continued to Bowlee and Birch.

The same view some eighty years later. Albert Turner owned the car and the shop, which was known as 'The Muffin Shop' by the children from nearby Durnford Street and Queen Elizabeth's schools.

New Jerusalem church, Wood Street. Mr Lister is on the left and Harvey Starkey on the right. The church was demolished and the coffins exhumed from the graveyard in 1978, to enable houses to be built on the site.

A New Jerusalem procession in Wood Street, with the day school top left and the church on the right. Mr and Mrs Barker are in the doorway on the left. Higher Cross Street can just be seen going across at the top.

Wood Street, 1929, with a Holy Trinity procession. On the left is the former Burton's Mill, attacked during the Luddite Riots of 1812. Musket fire from the defending workforce resulted in the death of four people. Two Oldham rioters were killed at the end of Chapel Street, another lower down and the fourth, George Albiston from Rhodes, an innocent passer-by, 'bled to death on the highway' (Manchester Old Road).

A similar view, with smoke coming from the 'Blue' Dye Works chimney, c. 1960. Factory Street is in the foreground on the left and the Community Centre has replaced Burton's Mill. On the corner of Chapel Street is Pickup's cycle shop with Wrigley Motors opposite.

Kid Clough Dye Works. Water from springs on Springfield was culverted through Middleton Rectory grounds to the work's lodge in Sadler Street. The overflow then filled another mill lodge in Wood Street, prior to entering the Irk near Jackie Booth's Field.

Horses belonging to Jopson, Ashworth and Edmonds Ltd, seen here outside the Kid Clough Works, soon after the firm was founded in 1889.

Inside the Kid Clough Dye Works, where the dyeing, bleaching and sizing of cotton and other yarns took place. At the time of closure three members of the Ashworth family were running the works, which employed a lot of townsfolk. Local streets were named after Mr Jopson and Mr Edmonds.

Five
Top O'Middleton
and Around

The Top o' Middleton is a fascinating area to the north of St Leonard's church, with ancient wells and the former Barrowfields, marked on Hugh Oldham's map of 1762, giving rise to much speculation. A barrow or tumulus (largely washed away in the flood of 1927) was discovered near Chadderton Hall, this ancient burial ground being barely two miles away. The Union Street area was where the club houses were built by an early form of co-operative, enabling some silk weavers to own their own homes. Weavers' cottages were still being built in the Brassey Street area well into the 1840s, but by then some Top o' Middleton weavers were battling against poverty, as described by Angus Reach in his book Textile towns of Lancashire. Some abandoned their handlooms to work on power looms in cotton mills.

Land to the west of Rochdale Road was formerly a mixture of common land (enclosed in 1650), manor land, glebe land and the estates of Langley and Hopwood Halls. The building of the Langley Estate, after the Second World War, brought major change to a once rural area. Hopwood Hall, with its spacious grounds, was where Lord Byron completed 'Childe Harold' in 1811, maybe inspiring the phrase 'There is a pleasure in the pathless woods'. A path from the Hall led via Seven Stumps to Three Pits Field on the far side of Rochdale Road, where twenty cottages were built on the Hopwood Estate around 1830. They housed servants, agricultural workers, a blacksmith and seventeen families of handloom silk weavers. Somewhat unbelievably, in 1851, a family of eleven and at least one handloom occupied one of the small cottages. Six of the adults were weavers and two of the children silk winders. The Hopwood Estate was also well known for its coal. It was said that you could go away to Blackpool for a week, leaving your fire untouched and return to find the Hopwood Tops coal still burning when you got back!

St Leonard's church, looking east prior to 1868, when the old pews and galleries were removed by Rector Richard Durnford. The pews, for which parishioners paid rent, only dated back to the mid-eighteenth century; prior to that just the wealthy had such luxury of seats, the ordinary folk 'going to the wall' where there were narrow benches or standing elsewhere. 'The Parish', its local name, is famous for its antiquity. Part of the present church dates back to 1100 and it is believed a wooden Saxon church once occupied the site. In 1412, Cardinal Thomas Langley, Prince Bishop of Durham and Chancellor under three monarchs, rebuilt most of the church at his own expense. He also endowed the chantry with stipends for two priests to teach the youth of Middleton. Finally in 1524, Sir Richard Assheton largely rebuilt the church as a thanksgiving for the English victory at the Battle of Flodden. The unique seventeenth-century belfry earned locals this sobriquet, 'A stubborn people with a wooden steeple'. From 1812 to the beginning of the Second World War, a curfew bell was rung each evening from 9.50 until 10.00 pm (and woe-betide anyone who wasn't home when the bell stopped)!

Margaret (Peggy) Smith took this photograph, which has been christened 'Peggy's Ghost'. A careful look and the title is explained. The rector's vestry at the south-east corner of the church was built partially below ground so as not to obscure the south chancel window that now contains the famous Flodden memorial.

St Leonard's Square, on the sad occasion of the funeral for Mrs Irene Richards, her daughter Mavis, son-in-law Joseph Motler and granddaughter Ann, who were killed flying to Madeira on 15 November 1957. The pile of stones in the foreground was for the new vestry. (Reproduced courtesy of the *Oldham Evening Chronicle*).

The Ring o' Bells and Church Street, *c.* 1900. William Hulton was the licensee from 1890 to 1915. Jacob Hulton owned the little shop at the top of New Lane and the land behind the Ring o' Bells, which later became the site of Hulton Care Nursing Home.

The cannons, a familiar sight on the recreation ground on Clarke Brow, until they were scrapped around 1940, for the war effort.

New Lane, 2 June 1962, with the St Leonard's procession led by Arthur Fletcher (carrying the cross) and Mr Smethurst on the left. The gable end of the top house shows a cruck frame. Surely this example of early housing should have been preserved?

Another procession at the bottom of New Lane in 1950. The corner four-storey building was the Militia House built in 1776, one of the first of many leases granted by Harbord Harbord.

Cheapside, 1965, with Mrs Dale (wearing hat) whose husband Amos was caretaker, chauffeur and millwright for John Thorpe's Silk Ribbon Mill, Spring Gardens. Thorpe's manufactured silk ribbon for military and commemorative medals and for men's hatbands. Another silk mill stood on Union Street. The other lady is Mrs Doolan who lived at the Top Drum, Rochdale Road.

Cheapside, with coaches about to leave for the Brewers' Arms annual picnic to Chester and New Brighton, 28 August 1954. The landlord, Percy Hilton, is in the middle wearing a light jacket. Everyone is identified but lack of space prevents inclusion here. The Brewers' Arms dated back to around 1861 and it is now a private house.

The Wesleyan day school choir, by the Exedra and Staircase, Jubilee Park, 28 July 1909. This was designed by Edgar Wood. Unfortunately, the fountain disappeared without trace in the late 1950s (although it was rumoured to be in some councillor's garden!).

Church Croft shortly before it was demolished in 1956. St Leonard's church wall is to the left of the back-to-back former silk weavers' cottages and to the right a similar row of cottages is very close.

Morton Street Primitive Methodist chapel, 1903. It was known locally as 'Twenty-Four Steps' and featured in L.S. Lowry's painting '*The Chapel*', commissioned by Bob Smithies in 1960. The building is now a clothing works.

Brassey Street, showing the rear view of Nos 110-116, in 1963. They were built around 1850, with elongated windows on both ground and first floor level and without back doors. The first floor rooms were heavily joisted to bear the weight of the looms. Most of the Brassey Street houses had lights blocked up and back doors inserted in later years, as shown on the left.

Fitton's Dairy Farm, which stood at the junction of Stanycliffe Lane and Boarshaw Road, 1972. Outbuildings were opposite where the convent and church are today. After the Second World War, prefabs were built on the farmland and several houses now stand on the site of the former farmhouse.

The residents of 'Gibraltar' must have been eternal optimists leaving washing out during the 1927 flood! Flooding was common here and water would go in at the back door and out the front, but this flood proved too much. John Lee Fold can be seen in the distance. Access to the cottage was by way of a footbridge over Whit Brook.

John Lee Fold's last remaining cottages, April 1906. The date stone was 1735 and they were near an ancient corn mill, which survived until the late 1700s. Prior to a footbridge being built, Whit Brook had a paved ford in the Fold. These cottages were demolished in 1936 and the Cromer warehouse was built on their site.

The Card Room, Cromer Ring Mill, 1948. The mill, built in 1905, was the last local textile mill when it closed in 1981. It had the same design as the power loom sheds of the 1830s, with north light roof windows and saw tooth profile roof. Single storey mills were at less risk of fire than the multi-storey ones.

Little Green, showing the old and new bridge, at the time of the flood, 1927. In the distance is Tonge Vale Mill. Prior to being straightened, Hilton Fold Lane crossed the river some hundred feet upstream and was barely a cart track. A road sign pointing up Green Lane on the junction of Dale Road read 'Path to Royton'.

Moses Dakin's chip shop, perched precariously above Whit Brook on Boarshaw Road. The Dakins used to prepare the chips at their home on Old Hall Street, which also was a hostel for elderly men, and carry the chips in buckets to the shop. As there was no running water, the council eventually shut the business down on health and hygiene grounds.

A thatched cottage nicknamed 'Old Swimming Yetter' (Heater) on the road to Bowlee, 1859. It was a drinking house or 'hush shop', selling beer and spirits 'on the sly'. Langley Brook once overflowed causing furniture to float around, including a heater used in laundering linen, hence the name. Others maintained the flood was caused by the quick disposal of drink when police were rumoured to be near!

Booth's Farm, Langley Lane. The four photographs on these two pages are from the 'Views of Middleton, 1856-1886'. The rare 'views', many taken by the Jackson Brothers, were incorporated into vellum bound albums, which were presented to families such as the Hopwoods and Mellalieus.

Langley Hall, the reputed birthplace of Cardinal Thomas Langley, who was born just after the Early English Hall was rebuilt around 1358. In 1466 it was sold to the Radcliffes of Foxdenton Hall and was demolished in 1885, when a farmhouse was built using some of the old materials.

Cottages on Langley Lane, with Langley Brook on the left. The lane has since been straightened but part of the old course can still be seen on the north side of the present road, near where the brook enters a culvert.

Manchester City Council built the Langley Estate, as one of its overspill estates. Some of the flats and the Gay Gordon are seen here around 1980, during the Langley Carnival, a major annual event for many years. Sheila Langton is in the Wilson's Brewery vintage dray, collecting money for charity.

Hollin Lane, Top O' Yebbers (Hebers), Whit Saturday 1953. The Hebers' Methodist church procession are just passing the old Gardeners' Arms. The road was once known as Hebers, becoming Heywood New Road after the modern road was constructed through to Heywood. It was not until the 1960s that the entire road became Hollin Lane.

The funeral of Mr Harry Bromley, headmaster of Queen Elizabeth Grammar school, October 1936. He was fifty-two years old and lived at 87 Hollin Lane. Middleton Billposting Company owned the advertising hoardings at the bottom of Hollin Lane.

John Tonge, a miser, lived here until the 1880s. The property stood at the junction of Rochdale Road and Hollin Lane. Frederick Harrison and his family are seen here, a few years later. The house was demolished around 1905.

The original Black Bull, 1892. This was mentioned in the *Manchester Mercury* as early as 1760. It was sold to Phoenix Brewery, Heywood, in 1889, the year in which Joseph Mills was convicted for selling adulterated whisky. The Mills also farmed and were sometimes fined for allowing animals to stray onto Boarshaw Road. The present building opened in 1893.

Edmund and Sarah Howarth and family of Yew Tree Farm, outside nearby Hatters Cottage, Stott Lane, formerly the School House, c. 1876. Sarah's father was John Kay, who farmed at Hatters Farm. Legend has it that Edmund's death from pleuro-pnemonia four years later was due to exposure, after some men he had previously caught poaching on the Hopwood Estate threw him over a hedge late one winter's evening.

Cooper Fold Cottages, on the former Hopwood Estate. In 1841 there were silk weavers and a huntsman living here. Cooper Street, off Hollin Lane, once led down to these cottages.

The Three Pits Cottages, 1967. Built for silk weavers, the cottages were around three sides of a court, with closets on the fourth side. Nos 10 and 12 were a shop and a beer house from the 1830s, later combining to become the Gardeners' Arms. Magistrates closed it down in 1919 because the two front doors made police supervision difficult.

Hopwood Hall, where an earlier building dated back to at least 1277. The Tudor bay window with its sundial can be seen facing the ornamental garden. They were added to the half-timbered medieval Hall, along with other extensions over the centuries.

The impressive dining room in the east wing of Hopwood Hall, where the Hopwood daughters placed the portrait of Lord Byron. He was a much admired guest in September 1811, when settling family estates in Rochdale. During his stay he rode over to Royton Hall to see the home of his ancestors.

Another view of the magnificent interior of Hopwood Hall. Sadly the Gregg-Hopwood's two sons were killed in action in the First World War and by 1924 the family had left. This Grade II listed building is now boarded up and lies empty and at risk until a suitable use is found for it.

William Heap, handloom silk weaver of Stakehill, who took his last 'cut' (or piece) of silk down to Tib Street, Manchester in 1888. Many local farmers also had handlooms for silk weaving, supplementing a somewhat meagre income from the land.

The Brown Cow Inn, Stakehill, was one of two pubs in the hamlet, the other being the Rose Inn, which closed in 1919. Formerly a farm, the Heap family, who held the license until 1940, obtained a beer license for the Brown Cow in 1870. The building has had a chequered history over the last three decades and has been closed for several years.

Hill Bank, Slattocks, c. 1910. Residents pose for this postcard, and they would later buy copies they could then send to friends. The cottages to the right, Nos 814-818 Rochdale Road, had stone-flagged roofs, hand-made bricks and original wooden slatted or baton doors. They were demolished in 1957.

The Rochdale Road surgery now occupies this site. The Griffin family lived in the left hand cottage and the Whitworths, who had a handloom in the kitchen in their younger days, in the other, followed by a recluse, Miss Reynolds. Walter Wellens, joiner and undertaker, had a workshop at the rear.

The Hare and Hounds, Nos 4-6 Rochdale Road, 1905. This was one of Middleton's oldest coaching inns, dating back to at least 1744. It served as a stopping place for both coach passengers and the York Mail Coach in the 1800s, when court leets were held here.

Idlers' Corner, Long Street, 1869. The cottages were home to the Haslam family. The lower one was so tiny that letters could be taken from the postman via the bedroom window. The gateway between the cottages led to the Tithe Barn in the rectory grounds.

The Haslam family assembled outside the upper thatched cottage, where they made and sold ice cream. Herbert (leaning against the door jamb) became a teacher at Durnford Street school. The site was cleared in 1925 and a scout hut was built on it. Thirty years later, S. Wellens & Sons built their present premises here.

The 1st Middleton Guides sword dancing on the field behind Idlers' Corner. King Street is behind with Cabbage Hall, dating back to the 1790s, halfway up on the left.

Middleton used to be largely agricultural and agricultural shows were held on Unsworth Hill, at the rear of the Old Boar's Head and on the field opposite (now Jubilee Park). This rare photograph shows marquees used for the show. Extra trains ran to Middleton Station to cope with the vast numbers of visitors.

Another early photograph of the Old Boar's Head, seen from St Leonard's Square. Unsworth Hill behind was levelled prior to Durnford Street, Grey Street and Sadler Street being built, with the earth being tipped into Kid Clough.

In June 1936 a flash flood caused the setts in Long Street to lift. These were wooden setts, often used outside schools to help soften the noise caused by wagons and horses' hooves. The National school, built in 1842 as the Parish school, was the inspiration of Rector Richard Durnford, who worked tirelessly for the people of Middleton.

After the service at the parish church, commemorating the coronation of Queen Elizabeth II, 1953, the Mayor, Councillor Arthur Horridge and council members march back to the town centre, passing Lancaster's 'Bottom Temp', Worsnup & Temperley, solicitors and Berry's confectioners (see below). The town clerk is Frank Johnson and the Deputy Mayor is Councillor Nellie Chisholm.

Inside J. & H. Berry's, bakers and confectioners, 46 Long Street. Mrs Berry is in the centre with Alice Nuttall on the left and Ann Band on the right.

The 1st Middleton Scouts parading up Long Street, 1952. Jeffrey Gillett is carrying the Union Flag and Harry Ogden (wearing spectacles), is on the right. S. Wellens & Sons moved from Back High Street to 54 Long Street in 1890.

J. Partington's shop, 7 Long Street, well known for its fish and poultry and the fact that the shop had no glass in the window. Bert Partington used to tell how children would ask 'Hey, Mister, were's yer winder?' and he'd open a box that doubled as a seat and reply 'It's in there'. Of course, they were wooden shutters. Bert's sister, Annie Butterworth, is inside the shop.

Six

Middleton Style!

Middleton had a distinctive style of its own, partly because so much of it was built between 1800 and the 1850s, when living quarters were basic and there were stone flag walls by every path. Here we have a glimpse of sights that confronted the clearance orders of the mid-twentieth century, when deprivation became an issue, houses with outside toilets being the main concern. There were 500 privy middens and 4,000 pail toilets in Middleton in 1891, mainly in communal backyards. The privy middens were earth closets that drained into open middens. The farmer milkmen would charge 6d, later 1s, to empty them and cart the earth away to spread on the fields. By 1973 all privy middens had gone and only thirty-eight pail closets remained, mainly in rural areas and by this time over 89% of the population had a fixed bath, hot water and an inside toilet.

We also look back, somewhat nostalgically, at shops that were household names before the Arndale Centre and supermarkets were built and at other features, such as the mill chimneys and Edgar Wood's memorable style of architecture, that were very much Middleton. The town was of course influenced by national developments, such as the coming of the railways, which offered trips to the seaside, the introduction of bank holidays and 'half-day Saturdays off' in 1871 and the inevitable souvenirs and postcards which followed (the latter being delivered locally before lunch time on the day of posting, such was the quality of the postal service).

A Hopwood Hall wedding at St Leonard's church, 16 July 1896, photographed by the Jackson family. Miss Judith Hopwood, eldest daughter of Mr and Mrs R. Hopwood and granddaughter of Captain and 'Lady' Hopwood is the bride and William Henry von Schroder the groom.

Frederick W. Jackson, a talented artist, was a son of David Jackson, one of the four Jackson brothers. This example of his work is entitled 'Sunday Morning' (Middleton Church). Fred was born in 1859 and worked in Wales, on the Continent, in Russia, North Africa and finally with the Staithes' Group in North Yorkshire. He died at Park House, Long Street, in 1918.

The Old Boar's Head, *c.* 1904. The property was photographed by Charles Jackson, another of David Jackson's sons, born in 1858. Prints were mounted on a single-sided greetings card and sent out as Christmas cards by Mr and Mrs Chas. A. Jackson, Market Place.

Market Place with Turner's Garretts (see also page 12) on the right and the Masons' Arms on the left, another example of a Jackson card. The snowploughs had not yet come out!

The Unitarian church, Manchester Old Road and Lime Street, designed in 1891 by Edgar Wood, whose family were Unitarians. The outside was austere but the interior was richly decorated, including a mural 'Seed-time and Harvest' painted by Wood in conjunction with his friend F.W. Jackson. The church closed for worship in 1960, was damaged by fire two years later and demolished in 1965.

Edgar Wood was an artist as well as an architect, with many of his designs supported by drawings now in the RIBA archives. This drawing is for the Williams Deacons and Manchester and Salford Bank, Market Place and it is signed 1892.

114

This postcard of St Leonard's church is one of the Harrison's series and among the very first to be published of Middleton. In a letter to the library, Alice Dean described how her father, Walter Dean (see below), photographed local views and Mr Harrison, who owned the newsagent's shop in the town centre, sent the negatives to Germany. The resulting postcards were a popular line in his shop.

William Cheetham's shop, Grimshaw Lane, with Walter Dean in the shop doorway, c. 1880. He worked at the grocer's, which was also a butchers, bakers and hardware shop for twenty-four years. He made his first camera himself, following instructions in a boys' magazine.

Not many homes had television at the time of the coronation in 1953, but these passers-by are able to watch it (in black and white of course) in Horridge's window, Old Hall Street (see also page 2). Even a passing policeman manages a quick look! It was the end of an era when the shop closed in 2001.

Inside Horridge's shop with Joy Horridge (later Lucas) and Graham Eadie.

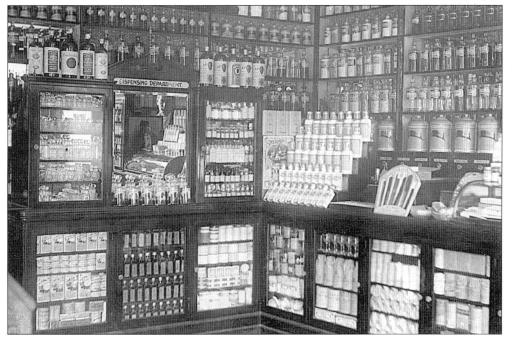

Sencicle's Chemists, 27 Long Street, opened by newly qualified Fred Sencicle in 1903. Following the shop's demolition to make way for the new Co-op store, the business moved down to No. 13. Two of Fred's daughters were teachers, Winnie at Durnford Street and Marjorie at Boarshaw.

The clock on the Central Co-op Stores, Long Street, bore the name 'Smiths, Derby'. The Co-op was of major importance in the town, covering virtually every commodity and service and of course the 'divvy' encouraged Middletonians to do their shop there.

Sadly the Co-op's prosperity did not last. Middleton Junction, along with other branches, announces that closure will take effect 1 July 1978, partly due to the amalgamation of the Middleton and Oldham Co-op Societies. Now only the Co-op funeral department remains in Middleton.

Thomas Thorpe, who raised his 'Lord Suffield' apple in his garden, at the top of Boardman Lane, Rhodes, in 1831. It was voted the country's most popular cooking apple at the National Apple Congress in 1883 and was included in Dr Hogg's 'Manual of Fruit'. He also advised Lord Suffield, who had an orchard attached to Middleton Hall, the town being well known for its orchards.

Commemorative pottery of Middleton. The Victorians' scant leisure time increased with the introduction of bank holidays and half-day Saturdays, horizons also broadening with railway travel available. W.H. Goss started producing crested china souvenirs in 1883, costing about 1s, with agents in many areas, mainly targeting the new day-trippers. Goss examples are seen here, with a Hopwood Hall cup made for A. Stevenson, Middleton and a Grafton teapot of St Leonard's, both the latter being parts of sets.

King Street, April 1965, showing the rear view of Nos 4-8 and the back door of the former White Horse, 74 Long Street. The tin bath, dolly tub, mangle and buckets were vital necessities, along with a blower, used to create a draught by placing it in front of the fire.

Washday in Ashton Lane (left) and Tetlow Street (right), 1964. Tin bath and dolly tub are again to hand but the old slopstone sink (extreme left) now houses a miniature garden. Notice the small cobbles, used in many of Middleton's yards and lanes, the stones being taken from local streams.

Schofield's Buildings, between Chapel Street and Kid Street (right), with Sadler Street in the foreground and Market Street behind, 1956. Scenes like this, with approximately thirty houses sharing the block of six privies, were the main targets of the clearance orders.

The toilets were also often targets for childhood pranks. One was to push a lighted newspaper or firework through the vent whilst the toilet was occupied, presumably causing quite a commotion! Another trick was sticking a drawing pin on the latch and smearing it with dog dirt – rather unpleasant.

Many homes had a cast iron range; this one was in a cottage at Boarshaw, built in 1914. Families would cluster around the fire grate for warmth and light and of course all the cooking, water heating, kettle boiling and clothes drying was accomplished here too. Disadvantages included the cleaning out and black leading!

A typical scene in a two-up, two-down, 1966. The back living room has a shallow slopstone, gas geyser, shaving mirror and a curtain to cover unmentionables. There was often a toilet roll, or newspaper torn into about six-inch square pieces, hung on a nail ready to take to the outside toilet.

Alfred Butterworth of Park Side Farm. Prior to milk being delivered in bottles, it used to arrive in churns, ready to be ladled into the customer's own jugs. The latter were then covered with a muslin, often edged with coloured wooden beads to weigh it down. The horses, knowing the round as well as the farmers, would move on to the next house of their own accord.

An Empire Day celebration, Durnford Street. Abel Wolstenholme, the Rhodes photographer, took both photographs on this page.

Middleton Market, Fountain Street, June 1968, where Pessagno's ice-cream van could be seen every Friday from the 1940s. Pessagnos began the business in Ancoats in 1878, joining up with Victor Maggi at Home Farm Dairy, Alkrington Hall, in 1957. Edgar Wood's father, Alderman T. B.Wood JP, owned Park Mill behind.

Silcock's Pleasure Fair, 18 May 1976. Some may remember the Wakes Fairs with Mitchell's galloping horses, Wall's Ghost Show, boiled sweets, toffee apples, black peas, small toys etc. Formerly held in Market Place, then Jackie Booths Field, this is on the former site of the Albany Mill, before the Ellis Factory was built.

Rhodes Chimney. If you mentioned Middleton, most folk in surrounding towns knew it by its large chimney, deemed to be the highest in Europe. Chopin, a friend of Salis Schwabe, admired it during a stay with the Schwabes in 1848. It really was spectacular!

Holy Trinity, Parkfield Boys' Brigade annual procession in Long Street. Processions were always popular attractions, bringing out hoards of people to watch. They are much less common these days.

The mill chimneys of Middleton, as seen from St Leonard's churchyard in 1959. Church Croft (see also page 91) is in the foreground. The chimneys of the Rex, Soudan and Don Mills are to the left, the Cromer Mill is in the middle and on the right is the chimney shared by the Baytree and Laurel Mills.

Coronation Day, 1953, where the book started, with a procession attracting onlookers as it passes Seager's Stores, Nos 76-78 Manchester Old Road.

Index